CW01582801

This Walker book belongs to

For Drew. We thank the universe for sending
your stardust our way. Mummy and Daddy
love you eternally. xx – J.W. & M.B.

For Siriol and Anwyn, my Bunny and Moo – O.S.

To Harry and Evie – H.S.

First published 2023 by Walker Books Ltd, 87 Vauxhall Walk, London SE11 5HJ

2 4 6 8 10 9 7 5 3 1

Text © 2023 Owen Sheers
Illustrations © 2023 Helen Stephens

The right of Owen Sheers and Helen Stephens to be identified as author and illustrator respectively of this work has been asserted in accordance with the Copyright, Designs and Patents Act 1988

This book has been typeset in Garamond

Printed in China

All rights reserved. No part of this book may be reproduced, transmitted or stored in an information retrieval system in any form or by any means, graphic, electronic or mechanical, including photocopying, taping and recording, without prior written permission from the publisher.

British Library Cataloguing in Publication Data: a catalogue record for this book is available from the British Library

ISBN 978-1-5295-0000-4

www.walker.co.uk

WALKER BOOKS
AND SUBSIDIARIES
LONDON • BOSTON • SYDNEY • AUCKLAND

DREW, MOO and BUNNY, too

OWEN SHEERS

WITH JON WRIGHT & MELANIE BARKER

Illustrated by HELEN STEPHENS

THERE ONCE,
in a bedroom
in the middle of a house
in the middle of a village
in the middle of Wales,
lived a boy named Drew,

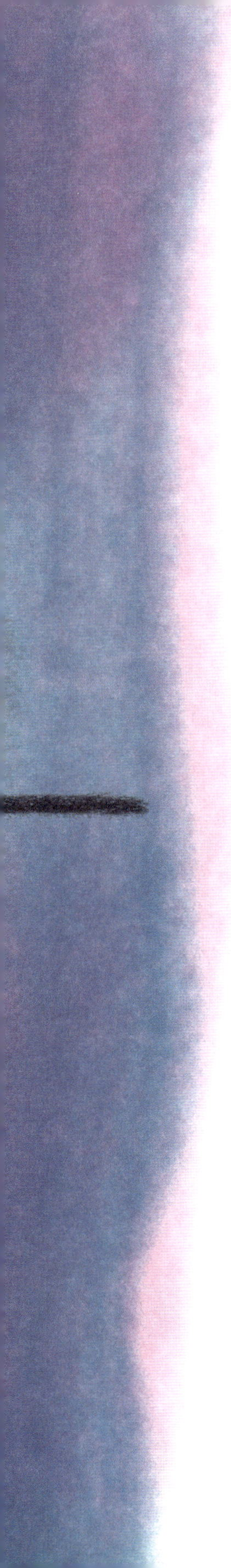

with two best friends,
one called Bunny –
who was big and loud and somewhat jumpy –
and one called Moo –
who was small and wise and somewhat floppy.
Now by day, these three best friends,
this close-knit crew of one plus two,
liked to play, as best friends do,
on a rug of red in their bedroom.
But by night, well, here's the thing.
By night – I promise it's true –
by night, the three of them, on that rug of red,
        holding hands, closing eyes,
breathing in then out in one shared sigh,
by night, you see, these three,
                        they flew.

Yes, you heard me.
Over land and sea, hill and valley, hamlet and city,
on that rug of red, Drew, Moo and Bunny, too,
flew and flew and flew.

Where to?

Oh, to lands unknown to me and you.
To night-time shores.
Midnight towns.
Moonlit isles.
Starlit seas.
Places that could only be reached
with a hand in a paw in a hoof in a hand,
with Bunny the one to urge them on –
"Down there! Into that volcano!"
or
"Swoop up now, over that hill!" –
while wise, quiet Moo would sit at Drew's shoulder,
offering her advice with careful caution.

"There," she'd say calmly. "Among those waves, look,
a blue whale's moonlit fountaining spout."

Or,

"Down there, in the middle of those trees, you see?
A tiger's bright eye and, lying just beside,
her newborn cub, only minutes alive."
And so, in this way, the three friends would share
the beauty they saw from the night-time skies,
keeping the treasures of all those adventures
not in a box or a phone or a book
but in the memories they made
in their three-as-one being, their three-as-one look.

Until…
One night, as they flew and flew,
Moo and Bunny and Drew, quite suddenly,
argued.

Bunny, you see, was hungry (as bunnies often are)
so wanted to fly to the East
to find something to eat – sweet berries, fresh leaves,
some carrot and dumplings stew.

But Moo, well, she was so loving how they flew –
the air in her ears, the stars,
the moon, the whole wide view –
she didn't want to stop or turn around
but just go on and on until the rising of the sun.

"East," said Bunny.
"On," said Moo.
"Please," said Drew.
"Please don't argue."

But still they continued, with their “East” and their “On”,
with their talking not listening,
until Drew, sat between them,
peered over the edge of their rug and said,
“Is it just me or are we much closer … yes,
so much closer,
to the sea?”

Bunny looked down. So did Moo.
“Oh,” they both said.
Because yes, it was true.
Their rug of red had slowed right down
and now was sinking, plunging through
the rushing air,
until…

PLOP!

It dropped them all, those three,
right in the middle of the very wet,
the very surging,
the very swelling,
enormous,
deep,
unknowable sea.

"Oops!" said Bunny.
"Oh dear," said Moo.
They looked at Drew – their child, their friend,
the only one who had ever made
a three from their two.
"Whatever, dear Drew," said Moo.
"Whatever – considering the vastness of this sea,
its waves, its forever-just-water view,
its deep, deep
depths –
shall we do?"

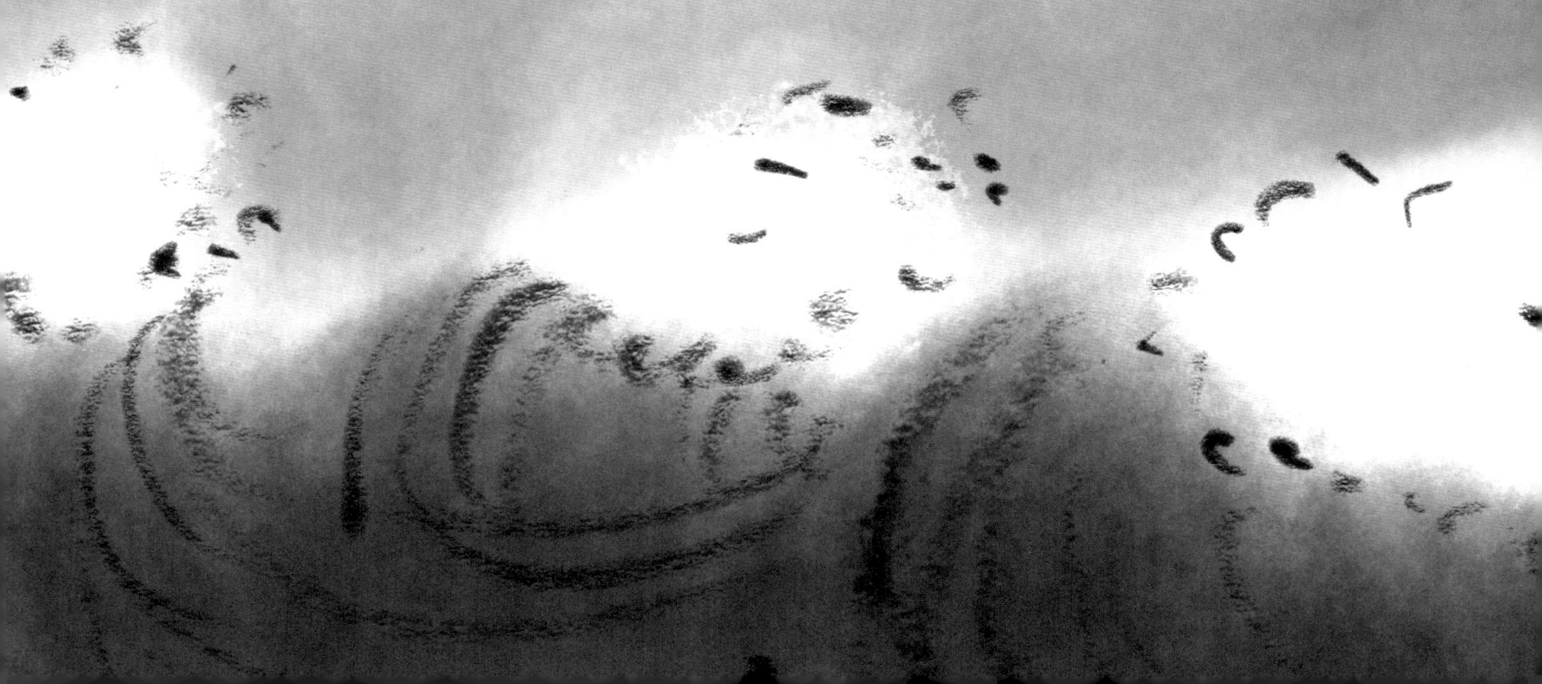

Drew looked at the rug on which they sat,
all soaked and furled,
and then at Bunny and Moo,
his very best friends in the whole wide world.
Indeed, he thought. What shall we do?

He looked further out, beyond Bunny and Moo,
over the swelling waves, the spraying foam,
and on again towards the horizon,
so far away yet all around them,
with nothing, yes nothing upon it,
no sign of tree or hill or land.

He looked harder again and harder still, and,
who knows? Maybe with that looking,
Drew made, as we sometimes can,
what happened next

happen.

2

A SPECK.

No more.
But there.
A dot
on that wide horizon.
An almost nothing, but yes, a something –
a single stitch between the sky and sea.
"Look," Drew said, pointing.
"What might that over there
be?"

They all looked together at that something,

that tiny speck of … what exactly?
Not land, but something else entirely
and coming closer now – surging towards them over the water,
pushing at the waves, the spray
and, as it did, growing so much larger
until in no time at all it was there –
three sails, three masts,
a flag proudly flying,
pushing on with a roll and a pitch,
a rise and dip,
a huge, towering,
wooden and iron
pirate ship.
Oh yes.

No national colours on this flapping flag,
no fluttering standard of a king or a queen.
No coat of arms above the waves, the foam –
just a square of black, like the deepest night,
and there at its middle in brightest white,
a smiling skull,
and, beneath its grin, roughly sewn,
two large and long
crossing bones.

So was this rescue or deeper trouble?
        Bunny and Moo looked up at Drew
        but how could he know?
Whichever, though, it was there, above them,
        rocking on the swell with creaks and groans,
and, dropping to them now, down its barnacled hull
(a sentence of fate or a glimmer of hope?),
a ladder of knotted,
        seaweed-choked
                rope.

The ladder stopped, then swung,
keeping a rhythm with the swirling sea.
Bunny gulped. Moo did, too.
"What," she whispered, "should we do?"

Drew looked up the ladder to the ship beyond
but there was no one on board.

No face nor voice from over the side.
But neither was there anyone anywhere,
all across that vast and surging sea,
so, giving his friends a smile
(more for himself than for them),
Drew took a deep breath
and, without a look to side or behind,
took hold of that ladder, tied on the rug,
then hand over hand,
foot over foot,
climbed.

Until…

THUMP.

He landed on the deck of that one-time speck,
now mysterious ship, uncrewed (or so it seemed),
that had appeared from nowhere, like a thought, a dream.

"Um?" said a voice from down below –
the anxious tones of little Moo. "Shall we come?"
"Or" – this was Bunny now, shouting so much louder,
over the waves, the spray – "should we stay?
Only, you see, I think we're sinking – slowly –
but yes, still sinking nonetheless."
Drew looked over and saw what he meant –
the rug wouldn't float with them upon it.
"Hold on!" Drew said (or, rather, shouted
because the wind, as I mentioned, was very strong).
"Hold on to the bottom rung!
And you, dear Moo, hold on to Bunny, too."

And so they did, and once they had,
Drew pulled with all his might,
hand over hand,
until…

THUMP.

All three were together once more.
Hooray! Drew, Moo and Bunny, too,
out of that vast, unknowable sea
and safe in … well,
where exactly?
An empty vessel – and a pirate's no less,
with a flag of bones in black and white,
with –
hold on.
Did I say empty?

Really?
If so, then what's that?
Over there, beyond the barrels.
Yes, there, I'm sure.
And again.
A hat.
And, below it, an eye,
and, next to that,
another, patched.
And, below them both,
a twitching nose,
and, below that nose,
a grim-set mouth.

Drew, Bunny and Moo froze –
and so did the face beneath that hat.
Three pairs of eyes met one, unpatched,
but no one spoke –
except the wind and the salt
playing their tunes on the sails
and the ropes –
until, at last, clearing his throat,
Drew summoned his courage and said, "Um?"
Then, holding a paw and a hoof
of his very best friends
to make him brave as they always had,
"Hello?"
The eye beneath that hat didn't blink.
And neither, Drew could bet, did the one beneath the patch.
The wind howled,
the sea surged,
but across that whole expanse of deck,
not a single whispered word.
Until…

Suddenly, and from the very air it seemed,
they all – men, women, three cats and a dog –
appeared!
Swinging on ropes, sliding from doors, rising from hatches
a rough, wave-washed, been-in-the-wars,
growling, snarling pirate crew –
and, at their head, leaping into view
and turning somersaults as she did,
the person beneath that hat – a girl, about the height of Drew,
all flapping coat and pistols and pockets and maps,
with a telescope of gigantic size,
inlaid with silver and studded with jewels,
loosely strapped and bouncing on her back,
as she landed –

THUMP –

right there on the deck
before the startled, gasping,
not-sure-what-to-do,
not-sure-where-to-go
Drew and Bunny and Moo.

SILENCE.

Just the wind, the sea,
the creaking of the rigging. Then,

“So…” said the face beneath that hat.
“This here is my pirate crew.
Now,
who are you?”

Drew, Bunny and Moo gulped as one
as every eye of that sea-salted crew
fell upon them.

“I’m Drew,” Drew said, his voice sounding small.
“And these –” here he squeezed a hoof, a paw –
“are my very best friends in the whole wide world,
Bunny and Moo.”
He paused, then, feeling braver, added,
“And who are you?”

An icy gust swept over the ship
as the girl raised an eyebrow
and, stepping closer, said quietly, carefully,

“Me?”

From behind her – a gasp,
as every one of that pirate crew
drew in a breath and waited
to see what their captain would do.

"Me?" she said again, a little louder this time.
"You mean to say you really don't know?"
Drew, Bunny and Moo shook their heads.
In return, she nodded hers slowly and said,
"Hmmm, is that so?"

Taking one step closer, she stood a bit taller
then tipped back her head and said,
jutting out her chin,
"I am Captain Jacqueline or Jack for short!
Famous across the seven seas,
the mystery of many oceans,
the queen of wave and swell!"
Here she paused and, leaning in,
asked, more quietly again,
"Ring any bells?"

Drew, with Moo upon his shoulder, leaned in, too,
and replied as kindly as he could,
"I'm afraid not, no."

Captain Jacqueline or Jack stepped back,
a frown now etched above her patch.
"Well," she said, "too bad for you.
Because if it had, then you might have thought twice
about trespassing here upon my deck!"

"Trespassing?" Drew said. "That's not very nice!
What about the ladder? The one dropped down the side?"

"Yes, yes," said the captain. "I know, I know.
But we had to see, didn't we? What you were,
and if you had, well,
something to hide…"

Then – as if that last word were a trigger –
she swung that telescope, so huge, so bejewelled,
up and over her shoulder
to land it clean upon her
unpatched eye
and looked at them.
Bunny, somewhat annoyed now,
looked right back in.
"Nope!" he heard her say
from the other end.
"Nothing – not a thing.
Get rid of them, me hearties!
Time for us to be moving on."
"Nothing?" said Bunny, affronted.
"Who are you calling nothing?"

Moo, meanwhile, at Drew's right ear,
was already whispering her hurried advice.
"I rather think," she said, "it's us, dear Drew,
who maybe should be moving on.
Wouldn't you say? Might we…?"

Drew nodded,
then shouted,

"RUN!"

And run they did – away down that deck,
sliding between legs, jumping over sacks,
ropes, barrels and kegs,
with shouts of "Catch them, catch them!"
coming from behind them, as off they sped,
with Moo, as ever, offering her guidance –
"Watch out! There's another! Go left! Go right!" –
and Bunny, as ever, urging them on –
"Keep going, dear Drew! Run, run!"

Until…
Skidding round a corner,
at full pelt, flat out, all three

F
E
L
L.

Yes, fell.
Dropped, all of a sudden,
their legs still hopping, still running,
down through the air and out of the light,
to land –

THUMP –

in … where?
Somewhere dark, that's for sure.
Somewhere under, not up.
Somewhere beneath a not-there-bit-of-deck.
Down,
down,
down,
in the belly of the ship.

Did I say dark?
Not quite.
For in that blackness were faint glowings of light
and movement, too –

shadows in shadows elsewhere in the room.

Did I say room?
No,
they could see now, Drew, Bunny and Moo,
that this was no room but a hold,
a vast wooden cavern where the ship's cargo was kept.
But if that was the case, then what cargo was this?
That moved and glowed and crept?

4

THE THREE FRIENDS PULLED CLOSE.

"I don't," whispered Moo, "like the look of this."
"Don't worry!" said Bunny, being brave again.
"We'll soon find a way out!"
"And how, exactly," said a voice from above,
"will you go about that?"

Drew, Bunny and Moo raised their eyes to the hatch
to see Captain Jacqueline or Jack, framed by her crew,
swinging down on a rope,
with a lamp in her hand, which she hung on a hook
as she slid on past and once more spoke –

"And why would you want to?" she asked as she dropped.
"I mean, just look!"
She swept out her arm
and, as if by command,

that lamp on the hook
burned brighter and glowed.
        And oh! What that light showed!
Such a collection, a wild compendium,
an eclectic, marvellous,
strange combination
of the all-there-are-few-of,
        the hardly-any-in-the-world-of,
small, large, animal, plant,
        loud, quiet, dark, fair –
a circus, a hoard, an ark no less,
        a natural bounty
        of the scarce and the rare.

A giant crab from Tasmania
with pincers the size of Moo.
A strutting peacock, a stone-still alligator,
a humpback whale in a sloshing tank –
all of them a bright, white albino.

In another tank, a sequinned squid,
and, in a cage beside, a golden tiger.
Next to her, the very last dodo
and, there in a jar, high up on a shelf,
        the ghostly green glow
                    of a northern aurora.
In another frozen, frosted corner,
Drew saw seven snow rolls
blown hollow by the winds of deepest Siberia.
Below them, a snow leopard lying on its side
beside an iced-over river of milky red water
and, above, in another large jar
(and drawing from them all a gasp out loud),
the birth of a rainbow,
        a stream of colours
                flooding from its cloud.
"How," Drew whispered, still drinking in
all the riches of that amazing hold –
the trees, the flowers, the petals and wings –
"do you find such wonderful, precious, perfect things?"

"With this!" exclaimed Captain Jacqueline or Jack,
pulling once more from behind her back
that giant bejewelled telescope,
shining in the lamplight all golden and black.

"A telescope?" said Bunny,
his ears half-cocked in curious confusion.
"No!" she corrected him.
"A rare-o-scope, my furry friend!"
"First," she said, whispering,
"this scope decides our direction
when, as I scan the horizon,
one of its jewels lights up bright
to mark the course towards something special, unique.
Green for a plant, red for animals,
and blue for wonders of the natural world."
Drew, Bunny and Moo leaned closer in.
"And then?" Drew asked.
"Then," the captain continued, "we follow it!
Our jewel-bright course,

each gem lighting up the closer we get,
until, when all of them are lit,
we are there."

"And then you take them?"
Moo this time, her voice
now laced with concern,
not wonder.

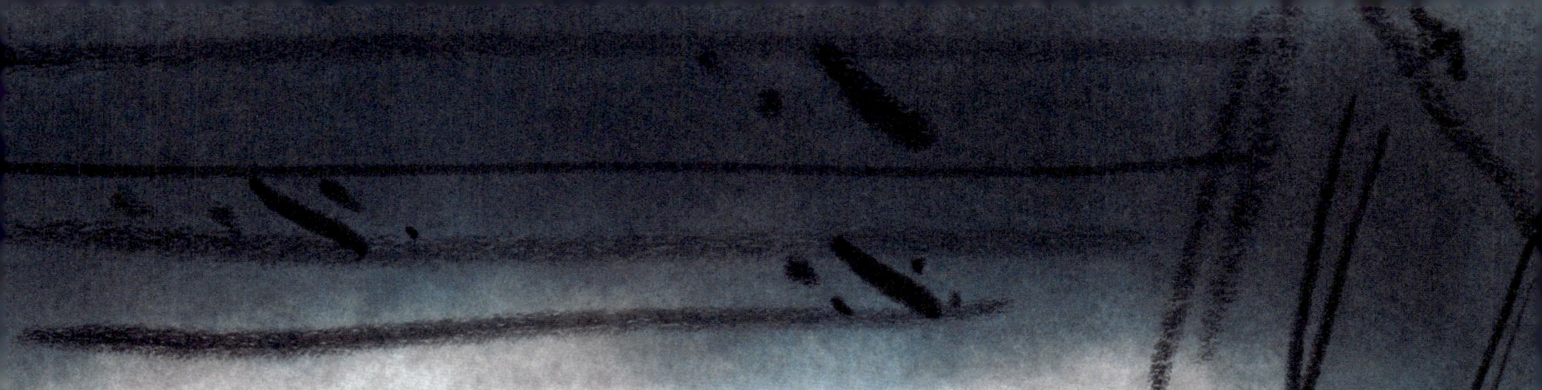

“Yes!” the captain answered.
“And keep them, too,” she added with a sigh.
“As you can see.”
“But…” Drew said, looking around them
at all that beauty hidden in the hold.
“Why?”

“Why?” said Captain Jacqueline.
And then, again, louder this time,
“Why?”
“Yes,” said Drew. “Why take them? Keep them?
They’re beautiful, for sure. But aren’t they better
left where you found them?”

Captain Jacqueline or Jack
threw back her head and let out a cry.
“Hoist them up, me hearties!”
And, before the three friends knew it,

quick as a whip,
they were tangled in ropes
and pulled up to land –

THUMP –

once more on the deck
of that swaying, rocking pirate ship.

Drew pulled his friends close
as Captain Jacqueline or Jack
came somersaulting from
out of the hatch
to land, one hand on the deck,
right there before them, neat as a cat.
"What do we look like to you?"
she said, pointing at Moo.

“Er, pirates?” Moo replied.

“And what,” said the captain,
“might send pirates across the seven seas?
What is it we’re known to go looking for?”

Here Bunny raised a nervous paw.
“Treasure?”

“Exactly!” said Captain Jacqueline or Jack.
“And what,” she continued, moving closer,

“makes treasure treasure? What gives it worth?”
By now, her nose was inches from Drew’s,

and her one blue eye stared into his.
“What,” she whispered, “makes us care?”

“Because,” said Drew.

“Yes?” said the captain.

“It’s rare?”
Captain Jacqueline or Jack smiled.
A flicker of a grin that grew

into a full-blown

B E A M

that spread from her face

to every face in her crew.

"Yes!" they shouted together.

"The unique!" cried the captain, dancing a jig.

"The one-in-a-million, the needle-in-the-haystack,

the one-of-a-kind, the joker-in-the-pack,

the almost-but-not-quite-

impossible-to-find.

That's why we take them!

Because being special gives treasure its worth

and these things we find, well,

they're rarer than any of the jewels on Earth.

And they're getting rarer, too!
Which no gem ever does.
So much of nature is! Disappearing, going, almost gone…

Which makes, you see, everything we keep,
year by year, become even more precious.

This," she said, holding the scope aloft,
"is what the rare-o-scope has given us."

"At least," she said, her eyes downcast.
"Until…"

"Until…?" Drew ventured.

"It brought us here," she continued.
"This spot, this whale-road back road,
this unmapped place,
where, all of a sudden, its jewels
went from burning bright
to dark, unlit."

“A false trail!” she wailed,
as her crew sighed behind her,
let down for the very first time
by their finder of treasure.
Drew, Bunny and Moo looked at each other –
the kind of glance that only friends know,
nodded, then looked back at the captain,
dejected on the deck.

“Perhaps,” Drew said, with a little cough,
“the trail you think was false is …

true instead?”

Captain Jacqueline looked up
and so did the eyes of her ragamuffin crew.

“True?” she said in a rasp of a whisper.
“How?”

"Well," Drew continued,
"we have something unique,
something your rare-o-scope might seek."

"You do?" said the captain. "But where?"
"Not here," Drew said. "Down there, in the sea.
The rug on which we were sat."

"A rug?!" said the captain, stifling a laugh.
"A rug, you say? Well, yes, now I see it. Quite a prize!"
At this her crew laughed, too.

"A rug," Drew said,
"that flies!"

5 THE WHOLE SHIP STILLED.

The wind dropped,
the waves ceased to splash and slop,
the very clouds seemed to freeze from East to West
as the crew stopped their laughing and held their breaths.

Until…
"Pull it up! Pull it up!" yelled the captain to her crew,
who, jumping to her order,
gathered their ropes and their hooks
and swung them over
to haul up that rug and land it, sopping wet –

FLUMP –

like a newly caught fish on the ship's wooden deck.

"A flying rug!" exclaimed Captain Jacqueline or Jack.

"How's that, me hearties?

A truly rare and special addition

to our wondrous, travelling treasure collection!"

Drew, Bunny and Moo gasped.

What did she say? An addition? To their collection?

Surely not. That rug of red, after all, was theirs.

Wasn't it?

Their way back home,

their past, their future, their safety.

"Oh, Drew," Moo said quietly. "She can't do that!"
"And she won't!" said Bunny. "Because you won't let her,
will you, Drew?"
They both looked up at him, with such trust and hope
that he knew, in their eyes, what it was he should do.

So, clearing his throat, he stepped forward firmly
and said in his loudest, bravest voice,

"Um, excuse me!"

"I think," he continued, "there's been a mistake.
Yes, we wanted to help, show you the scope was true,
but I'm afraid that no, that rug at your feet
is without a doubt *not* yours to take!"

His speech all done, Drew stepped back into line
with a now very serious Bunny and Moo
as the three of them waited, holding hands, paws and hooves,
to see what it was that the captain would do.

"I think," she finally said, all slowly and nicely,
tipping back with one finger her hat.
"The mistake, my friends, is all yours.
You see all of us here, we're a pirate crew,
and taking, keeping, it's what we do.
So, if that rug of red really flies as you say,
it belongs to us now, not you."

With a snap of her fingers, she signalled her crew,
who, as one, their smiles become snarls,
rushed on like a wave from the ocean,
their outstretched hands a rising crest.
Drew pulled his friends in.
He knew, this time, there was nowhere to run,
so, instead, he just lowered his head
and whispered to them.
"Don't worry," he said. "We're together,
that's what matters, so we'll be just fine,
rug or no rug, rain or shine."

He looked up – the crew were almost upon them.
"And thank you," he added, "for all the fun."
Bunny and Moo pressed into him, their child, their one,
and, closing their eyes, together they waited
for the hands of the crew to fall upon them.

But … no hands arrived,
because as the crew lunged, so did the ship!
A lurch and a swing, fast and then slow,
that sent those pirates tumbling down
as – with the crew scattered about the deck,
and Captain Jacqueline or Jack spread-eagled
on her back,

and Drew, Bunny and Moo still holding each other –
the ship, with water pouring from its hull,
began to rise and rise towards the clouds, the skies.

Thinking they'd been caught by a massive wave,
the crew braced themselves for its crashing down.
But no down came.
Just up and up.

The captain, on her hands and knees, raised her head,
her unpatched eye open wide in surprise.
"What's happening?!" she cried.

As if in answer, the ship swung again,
rolling her crew with their hooks and their ropes
off down the deck and, with them,
coming to rest with a clunk at her side,
the rare-o-scope with –
could it be? – all of its jewels
brightly lit!

The captain looked at the scope, burning bright,
and then down the deck at Moo, Bunny and Drew,
each holding the other in love and care,
and, beside them, their rug, still furled and wet.
And yet…
And yet…
Her ship. It flew!

In a flash, she knew!
"It isn't the rug that's rare, that flies!" she cried.
"It's you!
You three become one.
That's the treasure, what's special.
Your friendship, not some silly old rug,
that's what lifts you from below to above!
Your sharing! Your…"

And here she paused
as a word she'd never said before
came softly to her lips:

"LOVE."

6

DREW, STILL CLINGING TO BUNNY AND MOO,
took in the captain's words and saw that, yes, it made sense.
That's why they'd fallen from out of the sky –
because they'd argued, stopped caring, sharing.
That's why!

He looked down at his friends under each of his arms.
"She's right," he said. "It's not the rug that flies, but us."
Bunny and Moo looked back up at him.
"Yes," Moo said. "I suppose it is."
"Aha!" shouted Bunny. "Imagine that!
It's us who fly! Who are doing all this!"

"Which means…" Drew continued at a louder pitch,
as he got up and walked to the captain
still lying on the deck.
"If you keep us here, so will you!
And is that really what you want?
To be a sailor stuck up in the air,

not charting the depths of the sea, down there?"

The captain looked all around her,
at her terrified crew, holding on tight to whatever they could,
as the ship rose high and higher again,
up through the clouds and on into the blue.

"Yes," she said, dropping her head. "It's true.
Please put us down and we'll let you go.
I promise," she said. "And so do my crew."
"Hurrah!" said Bunny from down the deck.
"Oh, good!" said Moo. "Good for you!"

But Drew, he said nothing –
just stood there, remembering
all that he'd seen in the hold down below.
"Well?" said the captain. "What do you say?"

"What I say," said Drew,
"is no."

Hold on.
Really? Is that what he said?

Oh yes, and then…

“Not until you promise
to return what you’ve taken and kept.”

“Return?!” said Captain Jacqueline or Jack.
“Our treasures? Take them back?”

“Yes,” said Drew.
“To where they should be – out there.”
He spread his arms wide
to take in the world and all that’s beyond.
“They belong where they’re from,” he said.
“All of them. They shouldn’t be hidden or kept.”

"But," said the captain, "it's what we do.
We find the treasure,
and then we take it, too."

"And you can find it still," answered Drew.
"Just when you do," he continued, crouching down,
"when the jewels on your scope are all lit,
when you've drunk in deep on what makes it so rare,
then you can go
and leave it there."

"Leave them?" gasped the captain.
"But then how will we keep them?"

"You won't," Drew said. "But also you will."

As the ship swung higher again,
he laid a hand on her shoulder.
"A memory shared is a treasure, too," he told her.

"And sometimes more than the treasure itself.
To see in your mind how it felt to be there, together as one,
or to tell stories to others about all you've seen,
and in your telling make them care.
These are treasures you can always keep
and treasures, too, that no one can take."

"But our hold!" the captain wailed.
"Our years of precious cargo!"

"Your hold might be full but what about here?" Drew said,
tapping a finger over her heart.
"How full is this, after all the taking you've done?"
Captain Jacqueline or Jack looked up at him
and Drew saw, so clearly, the answer in her eye – empty.

The captain nodded – it was her turn to think,
as her ship rolled and pitched so high in the sky,
and her crew, all about her, shivered in the winds.
"But how," she asked at last, "might we return what we took?
It's taken us years to gather our loot.
We'd need… We'd need…"
Drew smiled and so, listening in, did Bunny and Moo.
"A ship?" Drew said.
"That flew?"

And so, dear reader, that's what they did,
that once-pirate crew.
Following the night and the light of the moon,
and with the help of Drew, Bunny and Moo,
across the globe they flew,
high in the sky above village and city,
returning the wonders of their stolen booty.

Some children, it's said, saw them go as they went –
the billowing sails of a pirate ship
in sharp and dashing silhouette,
as it crossed the face of a swollen moon
or caught the last light of an orange sunset.

But, if they did, that's all they saw – a glimpse, no more –
and then they were gone, off on their mission,
emptying their hold of treasure after treasure,
until, at last, only one was still left –
the same three friends with whom we began.

But then, as the new day dawned, they dropped them off, too –
departing with a wave, a thanks
and the tipping of a hat above a curl and a patch
as the wind swelled their sails
in a sandy little cove off the western edge of Wales.

Back on dry land once more, Drew, Bunny and Moo
waved them farewell, then unfurled their rug
and laid it out on the tide-smooth sand.

"Well!" Bunny said. "That didn't go as planned!
To think, we've seen the world in a night –
how beautiful it is, how big!"

"Yes," said Moo, stifling a yawn.
"I'd never have known. So many things to see, hear and learn!"

"So many!" agreed Bunny. "Shall we go out again?"
"Maybe," said Drew, who was looking sleepy now, too.
"But what do you say if we have a rest first?
Back in the warmth of our bedroom?"

"Oh yes," said Moo, settling down on the rug.
"I think Drew's right. We can go out again tomorrow night."

"All right," said Bunny, sitting down, too. "Ready, Drew?"

"Ready," Drew said as he sat down to join them.

Then, as they always had,

with a hand in a hoof in a paw,

all three breathed in then out in one shared sigh,

closed their eyes

and, together again on their rug of red,

gently, gently

began

to rise.

THE DREW BARKER-WRIGHT CHARITY

Funding research and supporting families affected by Paediatric Chordoma

Drew, Moo and Bunny, Too was inspired by Drew Barker-Wright, a real little boy who was diagnosed with Paediatric Chordoma, a very rare form of bone cancer affecting 1 in 20 million children each year.

Drew was born on 1st February 2013 and grew into an inquisitive little man, with a lust for life. He loved to dance, sing, swim and read books. He adored stories of great adventure and magical journeys.

This book is a legacy for Drew, a sweet and gentle boy whose journey ended at home, taking his final breath with Bunny and Moo by his side. Forever four.

DREW'S CHARITY HAS THREE OBJECTIVES

HELP FUND RESEARCH

To help fund research and the development of new drugs and targeted therapy

OFFER FINANCIAL SUPPORT

To offer grants to the newly diagnosed and to those families needing to make memories

DREW'S GIFT

To provide a bedside gift to each newly diagnosed infant in the UK

Drew's Charity is the first in the UK to specifically address Paediatric Chordoma. If you would like to learn more or donate, please visit www.dbwcharity.org

@dbwcharity @dbwcharity @dbwcharity

Charity Registration No. 1176680